SEASONS OF THE SEAL

A TRIBUTE TO THE ICE LOVERS

SEASONS OF THE SEAL

Fred Bruemmer
& BRIAN DAVIES

A LORRAINE GREEY BOOK

KEY PORTER BOOKS

Page 1: The mother watches nearby seals; the pup snuggles close.

Pages 2 and 3: An iceberg drifts slowly in Lancaster Sound in the soft light of the arctic night.

Page 4: Flipper marks and the trail of a dragged body mark the path of a female harp seal hitching laboriously across the ice.

Page 5: Of the tens of thousands of pups on the ice, the female (*left*) recognizes her own by smell. Sculling rapidly, another female (*right*) rises high in the water to look at her pup.

First Edition

Copyright © 1988 by Fred Bruemmer

Published by
Key Porter Books Limited
70 The Esplanade
Toronto, Canada M5E 1R2

Produced by
Lorraine Greey Publications Limited
Suite 303, 56 The Esplanade
Toronto, Canada M5E 1A7

Canadian Cataloguing in Publication Data

Bruemmer, Fred
    Seasons of the seal

ISBN: 1-55013-100-1

1. Harp seal.   I. Title.

QL737.P64B78 1988   599.74′8   C88-093640-1

88   89   90   91   92   5   4   3   2   1

Designed by Donald Fernley
Edited by Jennifer Glossop
Underwater Photography by Tom McCollum

Printed and bound in Italy

CONTENTS

INTRODUCTION

F red Bruemmer and I share a deep love for harp seals, and this book is an expression of that affection. It is a celebration of the seasons of the seal, in images only Fred, a superlative wildlife photographer, could capture.

My involvement with these animals has been a personal crusade against human cruelty. Hunted from time immemorial by native peoples living in coastal communities, the seals faced a dramatic new threat at the beginning of the nineteenth century when large-scale commercial sealing began in earnest off Newfoundland. This slaughter continued until the 1980s, by which time the hunters were concentrating on baby seals and had graduated from wooden sailing ships to sophisticated ice-breaking vessels. During this period, millions of seals were massacred, and the herds were reduced, according to some scientists, by as much as half.

I vividly remember the first time I saw a seal killed, on floating ice off the east coast of Canada in 1966. He was only ten days old, a little ball of white fur with big dark eyes and a plaintive cry. Playful, friendly and full of curiosity, he went to meet the first human he had ever seen. He was, by that same human, clubbed on the head and butchered on the spot. He was skinned alive. I saw the heart, in a body without a skin, beating frantically. After the hunters had left the ice, I saw the mother seal crawl back to the shattered carcass of her pup. My heart filled with sadness as I watched this poor, grieving animal. Great tears flowed from her eyes and from mine as I lay beside her on the ice pack, sharing her suffering. When the sun set on that awful day, I was deeply committed to ending the baby seal hunt.

For eleven years, full of the passions of youth, I fought the seal hunt. I fanned the flames of public protest lit by media coverage of the senseless clubbing, in the hope that a new Canadian law would stop the killing. In 1969 I founded the International Fund for Animal Welfare (IFAW), an organization dedicated to saving the seals. In 1977, older and wiser, I shifted the focus of my campaign to Europe, where I tried to destroy the main sealskin market. In 1983, in a humane gesture to public opinion, the European Economic Community (EEC) banned the importation of baby seal products. The seal hunt was effectively stopped dead in its tracks. But although

Above: The pup is curious and a bit afraid. Any dark form attracts it; it could be its mother.

Left: The seal hunt ceased as a result of a worldwide protest that was fired by images of the cute pups.

the press called the EEC ban a victory for the IFAW campaign, the slaughter was still not officially banned in Canada. There remained the possibility that new markets would be found and the killing resumed. I vowed to fight on.

In 1984 the Canadian government set up a Royal Commission on Seals and the Sealing Industry in Canada, with a mandate to recommend a new marine mammal policy for Canada. Even though IFAW submitted thirteen briefs dealing with the science, ethics and economics of sealing, I fully expected a whitewash. I was wrong. In its lengthy report, delivered in 1986, the Royal Commission made, in my opinion, a key recommendation: "That the commercial hunting of the pups of the harp seal (whitecoats) and hooded seals (bluebacks) is widely unacceptable to the public and should not be permitted."

On December 30, 1987, after listening to many groups (including IFAW), Canada's minister of fisheries and oceans, Tom Siddon, announced the implementation of this (and other) recommendations. And the baby seal hunt was officially ended. When I opened my newspaper on January 1, 1988, and read the headline "Canada Bans Baby Seal Hunt," it was a dream come true.

Accolades must go to Mr. Siddon for implementing a marine mammal policy that Canadians wanted. I could destroy the market for baby seal products and stop the killing at least in the short term — and with the help of many organizations and caring individuals, I did. But I couldn't dictate official Canadian policy. Along with others I could influence it, yes, but in the end, Canadians had to be on the side of the seals. Thank God they were.

BRIAN DAVIES

A hungry pup cries, hoping its mother will
hear it, return, and nurse it.

1
THE ICY CRADLE
OF THE SEALS

Two hundred thousand seals lie upon the ice in the southern Gulf of St. Lawrence. Prevailing northwesterly winds have pressed the immense ice fields of the gulf against the Iles de la Madeleine, the Magdalen Islands. The harp seal herd, a broad belt of scattered animals, extends over more than a hundred miles, from the rust-red Rochers aux Oiseaux (the Bird Rock which Audubon admired in 1833) in the north, to the sinister islet known as Le Corps Mort (Deadman Island) in the south.

The ice field in the southern gulf is bigger than Belgium. The large, flat floes are mat-white, separated by soot-black leads, zigzagging channels of open water. The seals, dark spindle-shapes upon the white ice, lie near the edge of leads or next to breathing holes which they have cut into the ice. Toward evening the wind increases and millions of tons of ice begin to move. Floes shift, leads close, ice grinds against ice and grates and groans. The pressure increases. Floes buckle and break. Dark water gushes up; broken floes slide over each other, giants in torment; huge sheets of ice rear up, topple and crash and are piled into ridges of ice. Ground ice and snow and slush swirl between the twisting floes. Above the din and chaos of the colliding and breaking floes rises the pathetic chorus of tens of thousands of frightened harp seal pups.

The wind abates near dawn, and the ice, so deadly in storm and turmoil, is suddenly still and sublime, aglow in the soft opalescence of morning. The newly formed pressure ridges shine in delicate lilac and rose, and milk-white icicles hang in grottoes of the deepest blue. Flocks of great black-backed gulls, winged undertakers, wail across the ice to find placentae, stillborn pups and the bodies of pups crushed by ice during the night. *Gull* comes from the ancient Breton verb *goelaff*, to weep.

Above: All innocence and large-eyed curiosity, a newborn pup has little fear at first. After a week it becomes more cautious and defensive.

Left: Harp seal mother and pup on the breeding ice in the Gulf of St. Lawrence.

To scientists the harp seal is *Phoca groenlandica*, the Greenland seal. Formerly it was known as *Pagophilus*, the ice-lover, an appropriate name, for this is the seal of the ice; its vast annual migrations follow the seasonal advance and retreat of the ice.

There are three geographically distinct and discrete harp seal populations: the Northwest Atlantic or Newfoundland herd, made up of the Front herd, which breeds on the pack ice off southern Labrador and northeastern Newfoundland, and the Gulf herd, which breeds on the ice in the Gulf of St. Lawrence; the Jan Mayen or West Ice herd, which breeds on the ice of the Greenland Sea in the general vicinity of Jan Mayen Island; and the White Sea or East Ice herd, which breeds on the ice of Russia's White Sea. A few seals with wanderlust may stray from one herd to the other, but both David E. Sergeant of Canada's Arctic Biological Station and his Russian colleague A.V. Yablokov consider these three populations of harp seals to be completely independent groups. But all met a similar fate.

The White Sea herd spends summer in the Barents Sea, feeding on fish and crustaceans near the edge of the ice in the vicinity of Spitsbergen and Russia's Franz Josef Land. In October the seals migrate south to the White Sea, and there, in February and March, the females bear their pups on the ice. Large-scale commercial hunting

After being hunted intensively for nearly two centuries, most pups are now safe in Canadian waters.

Ice floes shift. Leads open and close. In this moving, drifting world, harp seal mothers surface frequently and look for their pups on the ice.

began in 1870 and reached its peak in 1925. That year Russian and Norwegian sealers killed more than 500,000 seals. The White Sea harp seal population declined from three million in 1926, to one million in 1950, to 750,000 in 1962. It has since received some protection, and the population may have stabilized at 750,000.

The seals of the Jan Mayen herd feed in summer near the ice far north in the Greenland Sea, and the females pup in March on the pack ice in the region of Jan Mayen Island. This harp seal population was the first to be exploited on a large scale, first by whalers and since 1720 by sealers of many nations. (The whalers' main prey was the huge but slow bowhead whale. In slightly more than a century the Dutch alone killed more than sixty thousand. Now only a few thousand of these whales survive in the entire Arctic.) In 1774 the crews of fifty-four vessels from Britain, Germany, Denmark and Norway hunted seals on the West Ice. In good years whalers and sealers killed between 100,000 and 200,000 animals. Now this herd consists of between 500,000 and 750,000 harp seals.

The combined Gulf and Front herds were once immense. In 1760 a seal hunter of northern Newfoundland wrote that the migrating seals "filled the sea from the landwash seaward to the limit of [his] vision, and took ten days and nights to pass." Some scientists believe the harp seals of all herds may have numbered ten million before the hunters came.

Commercial hunting of the Front and Gulf herds began late in the eighteenth century and reached its peak in 1831, when 687,000 seals were killed. The famous Labrador medical missionary Sir Wilfred Grenfell wrote in an article for the *New York Evening Post,* "No class of mammals on earth has ever, or can ever, withstand such an onslaught." It lasted for two centuries, and altogether about seventy million harp seals were killed. It was surely the greatest, most protracted mass slaughter ever inflicted upon any wild mammal species.

In 1934, at the age of seventy-nine, Capt. Abram Kean, who had been sealing for sixty-seven years, returned to St. John's, Newfoundland, with his millionth seal. He was awarded the Order of the British Empire.

In 1986 a Royal Commission on Seals and the Sealing Industry in Canada found: "This hunt is widely viewed as abhorrent both in Canada and abroad." The commission recommended that "the commercial hunting of the pups of the harp seal (whitecoats) and hooded seals (bluebacks) . . . should not be permitted." The age-old hunt has ceased. Widespread revulsion has killed the market for seal products. Together the Front and Gulf herds now number about two million harp seals.

Left: Rain has washed away the snow; the pups lie on glare ice.

Harp seal pups
among ice floes
thrust up by
storms.

Just before sunset, a harp seal pup lies in
the path of golden light on the deep-blue
pack ice.

A fat and friendly pup rests in its bed of snow.

Following pages: Night falls on the ice and the seals. Females remain near their pups and nurse them frequently.

A two-day-old pup looks in wonder at its icy world.

A recently born pup, full of milk, lies blissfully near its mother.

The pup is hungry and impatient. It butts
its mother so she will turn on her side
and let it nurse.

2
IN THE WORLD
OF CRYSTAL CAVERNS

The spotted female harp seal is restless. With languid sculling strokes of her webbed hind flippers, she swims among the crystal cliffs formed by the storm-shattered ice. She rises in a greenish shaft of light to a hole in the ice, its surface quicksilvered by the sun, and breathes deeply. Another female lies with her pup near the breathing hole. More than a month ago she scraped the hole in the ice with the long nails of her powerful front flippers; ever since she has kept it open in ice that is now two feet thick, as a vital vent to the air above.

The female with the pup rears up, raises her head, scratches the ice rapidly and trills a warning to the trespassing seal. Like all female harp seals at breeding time, she is gregarious yet has a private sphere that none may enter. Sculling rapidly, the spotted seal pushes herself high in the water, stares with large, slightly bulging eyes at the distinctive silhouette of the threatening female, exhales and sinks into the cold emerald world beneath the ice.

The female glides effortlessly and surely through the stygian gloom beneath the ice (she can dive to a depth of a thousand feet). To navigate, she may – or may not – use echolocation. She does emit the distinctive clicks of echolocation, sounds that "ping" off their target, but, the British anatomist K.M. Backhouse has noted, she does "not have the enormously developed temporal lobes of the brain, the area responsible for acoustic analysis, as seen in the dolphins."

As she dives her pupils dilate until they are nearly circular. Her eyes are large and extremely light-sensitive. When she lies on the glaring ice of spring, her pupils contract to vertical slits. Her cornea has the same refractive index as water; within the sea her visual acuity is superb. A layer of silvery crystals behind her retina, the *tapetum lucidum*, amplifies all light received and reflects it upon the retina. Where a human would see little or nothing, she sees well enough to hunt quick-swimming fish.

Her long whiskers are marvelously sensitive. Receptor cells at their roots respond to the tiniest turbulence in the sea. A little crustacean jerks away; the seal's vibrissae, like sensitive antennae, detect the vibration, and she snaps up the tiny prey.

Above: A fat pup and its mother. The female recognizes her pup by its distinctive voice and smell. Pups, however, do not know their own mothers.

Left: Near its mother the pup feels happy and secure. When a female leaves and her pup is hungry, it cries desperately.

When the spotted female sleeps, she hangs vertically in the water just beneath the surface of the sea. Every ten to fifteen minutes, when her body's oxygen level falls, her brain sends signals to the hind flippers: they scull gently, she rises to the surface, the tightly closed nostrils open, she breathes deeply several times, exhales, the nostrils close and she sinks again beneath the surface, soundly asleep during all this time.

A splash wakes her. Another female frolics in the lead, swims on her back, snorts loudly, loops backward into the sea and surfaces again with a rush. The spotted female dives, sucks up crustaceans as she passes, and keeps gliding down into the darkness of the deep. Near the sea floor a sudden vibration alerts her. She snaps up the fish. Instantly she realizes her mistake, but it is too late. She has caught a sculpin, a big-headed bony fish, its fins armed with needle-sharp spines. The fish puffs itself up, the spines dig into the membranes of her mouth; she can neither swallow the prickly fish nor spit it out. She rushes to the surface, slides onto the ice and shakes her head violently to rid herself of her spiny prey. Finally she crushes the sculpin and swallows it. The fur near her muzzle is matted with blood, and she dives back into the healing sea. Somewhere in her brain a mass of information has been recorded, ready for split-second recall. In future, if she feels the turbulence signal of a sculpin, there will be an instant warning flash and she will avoid the fish that causes pain.

As she smoothly slides through the water, she leaves a trail of tiny bubbles that pop and click as she passes. Her incredibly sensitive ears pick up these minute sounds, as well as their echo reflected from ice that may bar her way in the dark or from the bodies of fishes that are her prey. (In a test, captive sea lions actually caught fish a bit faster in total darkness than in good light conditions. Some seals are completely blind yet are well nourished and fat and lead normal lives. A female gray seal I knew on Sable Island in the Atlantic came every year to precisely the same spot at the base of a dune, 425 yards from the sea. She bore her pup, raised it, mated and returned to the sea. She repeated this for many years. Her eyes were milky white; she was totally blind.) Sensitive to light and sound and pressure, receiving and analyzing the myriad messages of the sea, the female harp seal glides on beneath the ice, superbly attuned to her realm.

During World War II, when men were busy killing men and sealers and sealing ships were needed for the war, the seals had a respite. (The famous *Terra Nova*, once the ship of Captain Kean that took the explorer Robert Falcon Scott and his men in 1910 on their fateful voyage to Antarctica, sank in 1943 carrying supplies to U.S. bases in Greenland.) The scattered, broken legions rebuilt; the harp seal populations on the Front and Gulf increased to three and a half million.

But when the war was over, sealing was resumed with vigor and all the aids of modern technology: spotter planes that guided the sealing ships unerringly to the "main patch," the largest seal concentration; and strong, steel-hulled ships from Canada and Norway and icebreakers from the Soviet Union that rammed their way relentlessly

The female surfaces in her bobbing hole. Its edge is polished by her body when she slides onto the ice.

through the pack to reach the breeding ice. In some years of the 1950s and 1960s as much as eighty to ninety percent of all the harp seal pups were killed, as well as tens of thousands of adults. They were the cohorts of the dead, the age classes that never bred.

Responding to this immense loss, nature in some mysterious way increased the fertility of the remaining seals. In about ten years the females' breeding age dropped from six years to five years, and then to four years. (In the 1950s the hard-pressed harp seals of Russia's White Sea herd began to breed at the age of three.) Now that the hunt has ceased, the breeding age has stabilized, and scientists predict that as the herds increase the females' age of sexual maturity will increase as well. Harp seals live long. Females bear pups for sixteen to twenty years, and a few seals may live to be thirty or forty years old.

A harp seal hauls out to join her pup.

Rain and thaw that turn snow to chilly
mush and mat the pups' hair are hard on
newborn pups.

A sated pup clasps its bulging belly. It is
vital that the pups gain as much weight as
possible as fast as possible.

Full of fat-rich milk and happy with the
world, a pup plays contentedly.

Following pages: As wind sweeps across
the vastness of the ice, it shapes and
grooves the snow where the pups lie.

A female harp seal rises high in a lead
to look at her pup on the ice.

Adults swim and cavort in a lead. The
pups wait for their mothers near the
water's edge.

The kiss of recognition. The female sniffs
the pup to make certain it is her own.

Each female nurses only her own pup.
A pup that loses its mother is doomed.

3
EVANESCENT NURSERIES

T he wind has shifted to southeast. The pressure upon the immense ice fields eases. The great floes begin to pull apart. In the pressure ridges, huge slabs of ice tilt and crash. Dark water gurgles up, soaks into the snow and turns it to mush. Freezing fog oozes over the ice. Gulls rush low across the sullen lead-gray leads and pools of open water. Sounds drift through the clammy void, directionless and all-pervading: the snarl of an angry seal, the groan and creak of moving ice, the eerie wailing of the gulls, the cries of hungry pups. Into this shifting world of phantom gray, of ghostly shapes that appear and vanish, comes the desperate call of a forsaken pup.

The pup wakes up and finds its mother gone. It sniffs, it peers nearsightedly, but the mother, that great reassuring shape, is not there, and the pup is immediately frantic with fear. The pup is three days old. Without the female it is doomed. If a pup is separated too early from its mother, it will creep hopefully to other females, but they will roughly repel it, for they will nurse only their own young. The abandoned pup will crawl on, whimpering for food and warmth. It will sleep a lot and shiver, crawl feebly on and cry, sleep again, and die. "Nogg-heads," Newfoundland sealers called these spindle-bodied, large-headed starvelings.

The frightened pup shrills its pitiful bleat into the icy, pallid fog. Its mother surfaces in a lead nearby, recognizes the call and turns sharply. Her sculling hind flippers press against the water, and in one smooth, humped motion she glides onto the ice. Her long-nailed front flippers dig into the ice, and she urgently hitches toward her crying pup and nuzzles it. It is her kiss of recognition.

The female lies near the pup. It urgently butts her flank; she rolls on her side and the pup begins to nurse, eagerly, greedily, switching often from nipple to nipple. Drops of creamy milk dribble from the corners of its dark muzzle. Finally full, the pup rolls on its back, scratches a bit and wriggles, then falls asleep, a contented, furry, flippered blimp.

Toward noon the sun begins to burn away the mist. The freezing fog has rimed the ice and snow with large crystals which shine and sparkle in the sun. A rhythmic clatter fills the air. Four helicopters carrying tourists circle overhead, find a large flat

Above: The pups nurse frequently and grow quickly. In two weeks they triple their weight and double their girth.

Left: The birthplace of the harp seal pups: the ice in the Gulf of St. Lawrence.

pan on which to land and settle with a metallic whine. The brightly dressed tourists spill out of the helicopters, duck low beneath the whirling rotors and rush to meet their guide, a former sealer. They are fascinated but apprehensive. "Is there water underneath the ice?" asks a woman from Texas.

Guide and tourists walk toward the seals. Most female seals hump across the ice and dive to safety in a lead or enlarged breathing hole. A few remain, more than in former years. The older females lost most of their pups to sealers. Each spring men came and clubbed and skinned the pups, and these females vaguely associate the sound and sight and smell of humans with loss and fear. The young females do not know this fear. The guide stops near a female. She is worried but not afraid. She glides across the snow to the man and sniffs him, then slithers back to her pup who sleeps in a niche of snow. "She sure is tame," the former sealer remarks in wonder.

The tourists have come to see the pups, those silky white pups, with drooping

Tears run from a pup's eyes. Seals do not have nasolachrymal ducts; tears run down their faces and mat the fur beneath their eyes.

A pup in trance. Its heart rate slows and it lies motionless. As soon as the danger passes, the pup snaps out of its trance.

whiskers and soulful eyes, the eyes that moved a world to pity and ended an ancient industry. A newborn pup stares in amazement at the humans and creeps toward them, trailing its pink umbilical cord. Anything dark attracts it. It could be the mother, and mother means milk. It nudges and sniffs the boot of a tourist, then moves back, startled, repelled by the alien smell.

An older pup resists all advances. It snarls and waves its flippers. A tourist wants to cuddle it, touches it, and suddenly the agitated pup becomes totally still. It contracts like a frightened caterpillar, and a bolster of skin and fat rolls over the back of its head. The pup has fallen into a fear-induced trance, its heart slowing to fifteen beats per minute from the normal one hundred and fifty. The tourists coo and croon and pet the inert pup. It does not respond. But minutes after the humans have passed, the pup stirs and blinks, its heart resumes its normal pace, and it crawls away to shelter behind a block of ice.

At five o'clock the tourists leave. They must be back before dark. The abandoned pups are hungry now. The icy world rings with their cries. The females haul out, and the pups nurse with tremendous urgency. The whole mission of their little lives is to grow very fat as fast as possible.

Ice is an evanescent cradle. Warmth may melt it, currents may disperse it, storms can break and destroy the floes. In disaster years there is no ice at all. In 1969 and again in 1981 winters were mild and little ice formed in the Gulf of St. Lawrence. The pregnant females crisscrossed the vastness of the gulf with desperate urgency, searching for the vital ice, for harp seals do not breed on land.

In 1981 some females finally found ice, wet and broken, washed against the north shore of Prince Edward Island in the southern gulf. While horrified islanders and visitors watched and overzealous police and fisheries officers tried to prevent journalists and photographers from recording the spectacle, men rushed out on the ice near the shore and killed and skinned the screaming pups. (Sixty years previously, Sir Wilfred Grenfell watched the beginning of the hunt and wrote: "The slaughter of the innocents in Herod's day was as child's play to the massacre which ensued.") Few of these men were professional sealers. The professional is fast and deadly; a veteran sealer can club and skin a pup in less than sixty seconds. The amateurs who hacked away at the squirming, shrieking pups in that spring of 1981 near the shore of Prince Edward Island did a lot to halt the hunt. Films of this "hunt" so revulsed the world that soon after the market for seal pelts collapsed.

The females that search for ice can, in some mysterious way, delay birth by many days. But if they do not find ice, their pups are born at sea. The pups cry and swim feebly for a minute or two, then die in the icy water.

In normal years the females come to the breeding ice in January, and most pups are born in late February or in early March. They are thin and cold. Beneath the skin which hangs upon them in folds like a coat many times too large, the pups have a thin layer of insulating fat only one-fifth of an inch thick. They nurse avidly and frequently. The milk is creamy, slightly viscous and has an oily taste. (It is twelve times richer in fat than cow's milk and four times richer in protein.) The pups expand rapidly. Each day they gain four to five pounds until they look, as Grenfell said, like large butterballs dressed in down.

The pups nurse, sleep and grow. On windy days they look extremely sad. Wind-driven snow crystals and ice spicules irritate their large eyes. They become suffused with tears that roll in large drops down their faces and mat the fur beneath their eyes. Seals do not have the nasolachrymal ducts that transmit excess tears to the inferior meatus of the nose. (Humans have them; that's why we sniffle when we cry.)

When the pups are eight to ten days old, life is at its best. Some of the initial worry and anxiety is gone. Perhaps some instinct tells them that they have passed the period of greatest danger. Were they to lose their mothers now, they are fat enough to survive, even though they still nurse frequently.

The natal wool falls out in tufts, and the spotted, silvery-gray coat of the "beater" appears.

When the harp seal mothers hauled out on the breeding ice, they were swathed in fat. While the female feeds her pup, this blubber layer rapidly melts away. For every pound her pup gains, she loses about two. The pup's increased weight consists primarily of blubber, which, by the time the pup is weaned, is nearly two inches thick. This rapid transfer of the mother's blubber to her pup, via the fat-rich milk, is her legacy: a thick, protective blubber blanket which keeps her pup warm on the ice and later in the water. It is also a store of energy which will last the weaned pup for many weeks.

When they are twelve days old, the pups begin to shed their lanugo, the white, densely curled natal wool. ("Raggedy-jackets," the sealers called the scruffy, molting pups.) They are so fat and globular that their short front flippers barely reach the ice. In the less than two weeks since birth, they have tripled their weight and doubled their girth. (The pups of the hooded seal, which are also born on the ice of the Gulf of St. Lawrence, get even fatter, even faster: from forty pounds at birth they swell to between 120 and 150 pounds in just eight days.)

The fully molted harp seal youngsters are called "beaters"; their new fur coats are a smoky gray dappled with dark dots and rosettes. Later they become "bedlamers," immature seals, a word derived from the ancient French term for seals, *bêtes de la mer*, the sea beasts. To the first settlers of New France, as to French Canadians today, the harp seals were *loups marins*, sea wolves. At maturity the seals' fur is silvery gray with a spattering of dark spots which will grow with the years until they meld into black harp shapes upon both flanks. "Saddlebacks," Newfoundlanders call the mature harp seals.

A just-awakened pup spreads its broad,
webbed, rear flippers.

Crawling across rugged, slippery ice can
be difficult for a little pup.

Moist snow plasters the pup's natal fur.

Changing frequently
from nipple to nipple,
the pup nurses eagerly.

A young female watches
her first-born pup nurse.

A storm has broken the floes and piled ice into pressure ridges. Some pups sleep in the shelter of ice pieces. Others are crushed by the ice.

A pup watches its mother surface in a
lead.

Harp seal pups avoid the water until they are three or four weeks old. They lie near leads and bobbing holes and wait for their mothers to return.

Following pages: A narrow gap between the floes is crowded with male harp seals.

4
THE DANCE OF LOVE

Four times the spotted female has made the great migration to the seas and bays of the far north and has returned to spend the winter in the northern Gulf of St. Lawrence, feeding beneath the shifting, drifting pack ice. This year she follows an ancient call; she swims south in the gulf to the region where the adult harp seals gather. Although slow and heavy upon the ice, she is nearly weightless in water. She glides with easy, supple grace through grottoes of ice, some of which reach as far as fifty feet below the surface of the sea. She lies idly for a moment on a shelf of ice, then slides off and dives deep into the dark caverns of the night.

A lead just north of the main breeding ice is crowded with jostling seals. They are all males. Most of them are fully mature, eight years old or older. They are the same color and size as adult females, about six feet long and four hundred pounds, and all have jet-black heads and dark saddle marks. They are very noisy. They grunt and squeal; they bark sharply, gutturally. Suddenly one sends out a high-pitched, eerie trill that rises in intensity, trails off like a distant echo and abruptly rises again. The males are extremely excited. They splash and rush through the lead, threaten each other and even bite.

The sea beneath the ice is full of sound. Shrimps often snap and crackle, and some fish make a rasping, grating noise. Sound waves travel far in the water. The crunching steps of tourists on the ice are heard by seals beneath the ice more than a mile away. (In the Arctic the ice is six feet thick, yet an Inuk hunter poised with his harpoon over a ringed seal's breathing hole stands on a thick piece of caribou fur to muffle even the slightest sound, and the polar bear who also waits for seals lies soundlessly on thick-furred paws.)

The male seals are very vocal. They grunt and bark and groan and squeal. They have more than fifteen distinct calls; some are high-pitched and shrill and carry for more than a mile in the water, and others, in low frequency, carry even farther. (The humpback whale's low-frequency notes carry over enormous distances; the deepest, most sonorous may be heard by other whales in a sea area larger than France.)

Above: Marvelously graceful, a seal makes a loop in the water, surfaces and swims in the lead on its back.

Left: In the late evening a female casts a long shadow on the ice.

The spotted female hears the scrapping males. Their voices lure and repel her. She swims beneath the ice from pool to pool, tense and undecided. At last she joins the males, and in an instant there is a churning melee. The whole group of eager males rushes at the female. She turns and threatens them. They retreat, abashed. She flees and a dozen males pursue her. They turn upon each other in jealous anger and bite and scratch, then resume the wild chase beneath the ice.

She surfaces in a pool, and her throng of suitors surges up behind her. She rebuffs them and they fight. A few already bleed from deep scratches on neck and flank. The female dives again and leads them on. At last only one male, stronger, faster, more persistent than the rest, follows her. They surface in a large oval pool among the floes. The female slides onto the ice and immediately turns to watch the male. That is his signal. Now he woos her in a display of speed and passion and exuberance that lasts for nearly an hour.

An eager crowd of male harp seals awaits the arrival of the females.

58

He swims on his back across the pool and snorts and bubbles. He somersaults backward and comes up in a flash. He splashes and thrashes, then porpoises across the pool in joyous leaps. As his excitement mounts, he swims faster and faster, races around the edge of the pool, dives deep, rockets high out of the water and comes down with a resounding splash. Twice he swims to the female, but she pulls back from the edge of the floe.

As the male performs for her at an ever faster pace, the female, too, becomes excited. She slides restlessly backward and forward at the edge of the ice. She watches the male intently, and when he dives she dips her head into the water to see him loop and circle and somersault with marvelous speed and grace. She curves her body until only her front flippers and a small portion of her belly touch the ice. Tense with excitement, she flippers the ice, turns several times, then slithers to the edge of the floe and, her head raised high, watches the male with keen concentration.

He surges out of the water onto the ice near her. She recoils, but when he glides back into the water she follows him. He no longer chases her. They swim softly together, touching frequently, in a sensuous ballet of desire. He holds her neck and clasps her with his flippers, and they mate in the water at the edge of the floe.

About forty million years ago in the remote Oligocene, an otterlike animal took to the sea somewhere in the North Atlantic and became the ancestor of the *Phocidae*, the present nineteen species of "true seals." (Actually only eighteen are left. The West Indian monk seal, first described by Columbus in August of 1594 and once numerous, was last seen in 1952. It is now considered extinct.) At about the same time a bearlike animal that inhabited the rim of the North Pacific went to sea and became the ancestor of the "eared seals," the *Otarioidea*, the present sixteen species of fur seals, sea lions and the walrus. Over more than thirty million years they evolved separately but convergingly, perfectly adapted to life in the sea. The harp seals, with a population at one time of perhaps ten million, were among the most successful of the pinnipeds, the "fin-footed" tribe, and they linked their fate to ice and to the fish-swarming seas of the north.

Following pages: Steam glows in the red light of the rising sun on a bitterly cold morning.

The water of the northern seas has a temperature of about twenty-eight degrees Fahrenheit, but its thermal conductivity is twenty-three times greater than air. If a human is immersed in such icy water, his core temperature drops rapidly and he dies in about five minutes. The harp seal spends its life in these seas, oblivious to the killing cold.

The seal is built like a thermos bottle, its warm core surrounded by a thick, nonconductive blubber shell. A fine network of arterioles leads through the blubber and brings just enough blood to the skin to keep it healthy. While the seal's core temperature is ninety-eight degrees Fahrenheit, its skin temperature is just above freezing, and very little heat, or energy, is lost to the sapping sea.

To prevent heat loss from the large, broad-webbed flippers, arterial and venous blood vessels lie close together, like cables in a conduit. The warm arterial blood

flowing to the flippers is cooled by the returning venous blood. On days when sunshine warms the seals basking upon the glittering ice, the arterioles expand and an increased flow of cooling blood returns to the core. (When walruses that are hauled out on land get very warm, they turn pink or brick-red as blood flushes close to the surface of the skin to cool their massive bodies.)

The blubber keeps the harp seal warm. It is the seal's energy reserve. And it streamlines the seal's body so it glides smoothly through the sea. The Greek word for seal, *phōkē*, is derived from the Sanskrit root, *sphâ*, which means to swell, and reflects the ancient knowledge that seals are smooth-lined and very fat. The vital blubber layer, a soft and yielding cushion, protects the seals from the enormous water pressure of the deep and from the hammering waves that can buffet them at the surface of the sea.

A female raises herself on sturdy front flippers.

Surfacing in the harp seal threat posture, a female warns another female on the ice to retreat.

Blubber, transferred from mother to pup through fat-rich milk, provides the pup with vital energy and warmth. Except for three weeks of each year, an adult female harp seal is always pregnant. Her true gestation period lasts seven and a half months. But it is imperative that she have pups at nearly exact one-year intervals so birth will coincide with the maximum extent and thickness of the breeding ice. After conception, the fertilized ovum divides, divides again and again, and then stops. The blastocyst, still smaller than a pinhead, ceases to grow. It floats in its mother's womb, a mote of suspended life. Eleven weeks later, the blastocyst implants and resumes active growth. It is thanks to this delayed implantation that female harp seals can keep their date with destiny upon the whelping ice in early March.

Harp seals are the seals of the ice: they breed on the ice, molt on the ice and follow the advancing and retreating northern ice in their great migrations.

An angry harp seal mother clutches a
block of ice.

A raised head and a high-pitched, gurgling trill are the harp seal's threat signals.

A mother seal surfaces in a pool of crystal-
clear water.

The female dives, rises with a rush and
slides smoothly up onto the ice.

Her sharp-nailed front flippers claw the
ice as a female hitches toward her pup.

Ice glitters in the rising sun, whose slanting rays outline the seals in silver and gold.

5
THE WAIFS

The mothers have weaned and abandoned their three-week-old pups. The adult harp seals have mated and left the southern Gulf of St. Lawrence to swim northeastward. In the northern gulf they will feed and fatten again after the extreme stress of motherhood (some females have lost more than a hundred pounds in these three weeks). Then they will molt upon the ice before beginning the long migration north.

The pups are now alone on the ice, and for a while they are extremely unhappy. They wail and crawl upon fat bellies and search for mothers who will never return. "The crying of a herd of whitecoats is something not easily forgotten," wrote William Croaker, founder and editor of the newspaper *The Fishermen's Advocate*. "It is a pitiable cry, and it seems hard to slaughter those innocents."

Slowly they become resigned. They neither eat nor drink. Most of the time they sleep. Their thick layer of blubber, metabolized, provides them with both energy and water. At first they lie dispersed upon the floes. Gradually they crawl toward each other and collect near the floe edge in chummy pods.

After two weeks of fasting, the pups become hungry and restless. The water fascinates but also frightens them. They crawl to the edge of the floe, peer into the sea, get their muzzles wet and recoil. One pup, bolder than the rest, leans far forward, weaves back and forth, slips on the icy rim and tumbles into the lead. Terrified, it turns around immediately and tries to climb back onto the familiar floe, but the edge is high and slippery and the pup keeps sliding back. Crying and pathetic, it swims awkwardly across the lead, its head held high. And suddenly something clicks, the ancient knowledge of the tribe asserts itself. The hind flippers begin to scull in smooth rhythm. The front flippers lie in small depressions on the side so as not to impede the seal's smooth forward flow. The pup looks down into the water and sees a whole new world, the world of seals. It dives, a bit clumsily since its thick blubber layer makes it buoyant, comes up and sputters and snorts, and then begins to puff and frolic in the lead. It has found its true realm. Soon other pups, attracted by the happy splasher, slip into the lead. After a while they rush and chase each other, nip and tumble, then dive to explore the world beneath the floes.

Above: When the pups first go to sea, diving is a problem; they lack experience and they are buoyant and fat.

Left: Lost among the ice blocks, a pup cries for its mother.

It is mid-April now and the sea is stupendously rich. Mineral-rich water layers well up from the deep. Phytoplankton, sea plants so tiny that twelve million live in a gallon of water, thrive on the minerals and also convert the sun's distant energy into living tissue. They are the base of the mighty pyramid of sea life. A blue whale scoops from the sea each day two tons of planktonic animals, which in turn obtained that day through the sea's chain of life the food energy of five trillion sea plants.

The ocean meadows are in bloom. The sea is thick with life, and for the harp seal pups, life as apprentice hunters is easy. They simply swim along and suck in small crustaceans, mostly euphausids and amphipods, an endless feast of shrimplike animals rich in fat and protein. With the negligent ease of someone picking tidbits from a lavish plate, they feast for two or three weeks. Then one pup and another and finally all of them yield to a compelling urge to swim north and east toward the Strait of Belle Isle, which separates Newfoundland from Labrador. The great migration has begun.

When their mothers leave, pups sometimes crawl to each other, seeking comfort.

White hairs are hollow; their inner surface conducts solar heat to the skin.

Unlike adult harp seals, which are gregarious and swim together in friendly, talkative groups, the pups are solitary. They swim alone and in the dark (the pups migrate mainly at night and rest and feed during the day). At a steady two or three miles per hour, they travel through the Strait of Belle Isle and on across Davis Strait. In early June they will reach southwest Greenland, where they feed on the swarms of crustaceans in the fiords that cut deep into that magnificent coast. In the end, they will have swum across two thousand miles of sea to the fiords where their ancestors summered.

Many theories have been advanced to explain this unerring travel across the vast northern seas: that the seals are guided by the stars, by prevailing winds, by the salinity of ocean currents, by the position of the ice edge at that time of year. As yet, we humans do not know.

In the 1960s, when the "harp seal controversy" began to attract worldwide attention, with cover stories in such European mass-circulation magazines as *Paris Match, Stern* and *Epoca*, the most urgent question seemed to be: how many seals are there left? Seal protectionists spoke darkly about "extermination"; sealers and politicians claimed blithely that there were as many harp seals as there had always been. Both demanded a quick and definitive answer from the scientists of the hitherto largely ignored and badly underfunded Arctic Biological Station of the Canadian Department of Fisheries and Oceans.

The first aerial photographic surveys were inconclusive. The white pups just did not show up against white ice, and the females were not always with their pups. The next spring aerial pictures were taken with infrared film, which is sensitive to heat rays. This method was also unsuccessful. The pups were so superbly insulated by blubber and fur that they gave off hardly any warmth, and nothing registered on the film. Finally ultraviolet-sensitive film was tried. On this the white pups showed up clearly as dark spots, since the pups' fur absorbed light in those wavelengths.

A closer look at the pups' fur, with a scanning electron microscope, reveals that it is a most ingenious solar heat convector. The hair is not really white, but is a pigmentless, translucent structure with a core of such low density that it is nearly hollow. Light is reflected by the inner surface of the hair, which acts as a light pipe that transmits absorbed ultraviolet energy to the pups' skin. The fur produces a greenhouse effect; on sunny as well as on cloudy days the pups bask in the solar warmth collected by their fur.

This fur was the pups' curse but finally also their salvation. For their furs the sealers clubbed the pups, crushing the thin skulls, and then, with quick, deft strokes of the long-bladed razor-sharp knife, they took off the sculp – the skin and blubber. The men worked with speed and precision. In 1928 the crew of the *Bonaventure* reached the main patch and killed and skinned eight thousand pups "in a few hours before dark." The pelts were tanned and used as trim. In recent years, they were used primarily as "fun fur." The blubber was rendered into fine oil that was used to make margarine, lipstick, soaps, lotions and high-quality lubricants.

At last, their very beauty saved the pups. They were so immensely appealing, so white and cute and innocent, that to kill them seemed a sin. All other arguments lost strength before the emotional appeal of the cuddly harp seal pups.

The look of innocence that touched the world.

Following pages: Head held high and sculling awkwardly with hind flippers held far too high, a pup swims for the first time.

A curious pup fell into a lead. Now it
seeks help and support from its mother.

A drenched pup rushes out of the water.
Although their thick blubber layer protects
them from the cold, pups avoid the water
until they have molted.

A seal mother greets her pup off the coast
of Labrador.

To escape from wind and driven snow,
a pup has crawled into a cleft between
jumbled ice blocks.

Buoyed by a thick blubber layer, an
apprentice swimmer drifts leisurely along
the ice edge.

Pup and mother meet in the lead at the
edge of the floe.

6
FOOD, FAT AND NEW FUR

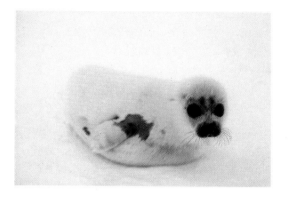

The storms of spring have broken the vast ice pans in the Gulf of St. Lawrence. The white plains of early March, seamed with soot-black leads, have split into myriad floes that grate and growl against each other as swells from the open sea heave and twist the ice. Ground ice, called "sish" by Newfoundlanders, fills the gaps between the floes. Each floe has now a pure white center and a raised rim of grayish, soggy, crushed ice.

Through this shifting, wind-driven, current-carried world of ice, the harp seals swim north and east. Those females that bore pups this year are now so lean that outlines of bones show through their thinned blubber blanket. Now all seals feed voraciously to replenish their fat reserves before the onset of the stressful molt.

The spotted seal surfaces in the mushy crushed ice between the floes. Shiny droplets bead her drooping whiskers. She peers around, sees only ice in all directions, exhales and dives. Her body responds automatically and efficiently. Her V-shaped nostrils shut. The pupils dilate, dark orbs sensitive to the faintest light. Her heart slows from more than a hundred beats per minute to less than ten. Muscles close the pin-sized otic orifices, but she nevertheless hears well under water. In water humans lack directional hearing; sounds seem to come from everywhere. The seal hears every sound with perfect distinctness; the bone structure of her head absorbs and transmits the sound waves.

She is as one with the sea, sentient to minute vibrations, to any sound that may mean food. She glides obliquely down toward the blue-black darkness of the ocean floor. A mottled, sand-colored flatfish, an American plaice, undulates above the sea floor, as softly as a feather floating in still air and yet not softly enough. The spotted female senses the faint movement, lunges and with one bite cuts the fish in two, then eats the floating pieces. She rises rapidly to breathe among the sun-flecked greenish ice floes and dives again.

Sunlight pours into the sea; winter's dormancy is broken by a passionate renewal of life. Diatoms, the grasses of the sea, each microscopic plant encased in a jewel-like silica shell, multiply by rapid division. Copepods, rice-sized crustaceans, graze in these infinite pastures; fanlike appendages swirl water and diatoms into their bodies. Each

Above: "Raggedy-jackets" was what sealers called molting pups.

Left: Seals at the edge of a slush-filled lead, a rift among the great floes of the gulf.

87

copepod swallows 120,000 diatoms a day. Schools of herring strain the myriad jerking little copepods from the sea with sievelike gill rakers.

Far beneath the schooling fish the spotted female, swimming slowly on her back, sees the glitter of the amorphous silvery cloud. She shoots up among the herring and rapidly snaps up fish after fish. The massed herring scatter and then regroup. The swirl of fish confuses the hunter. The seal catches a few more laggards and surfaces to breathe. She feeds for an hour and then swims northward again. The sea is full of seals, all swimming toward a common goal, the ice fields in the northern gulf.

The spotted female hauls out on an oval pan, rears up and looks around. As far as her somewhat vague, astigmatic vision reaches, the ice floes are speckled with the spindle shapes of seals. Her fur, so glossy a month ago, now looks dull and moldy, a mat, faded brown. The skin is scabrous and itchy. Small flakes of skin and hair peel off and litter the ice. (Homer, no doubt, had molting seals in mind when he wrote in the *Odyssey*: "Web-footed Seals forsake the stormy swell, and sleep in herds, exhaling nauseous smell.")

A great lassitude overcomes the spotted seal. She sleeps. She wakes briefly, yawns deeply, looks around with tired eyes and goes to sleep again. The flaking skin is sensitive and itchy. She wakes suddenly and scratches. The short foreflippers have no clavicles, but with their ball-and-socket joint are amazingly flexible. She scratches her neck and side and belly, swivels the flipper and scratches her back. She rubs and rolls and twists upon the ice and, suddenly exhausted, slumps and sleeps again.

Slowly, dead skin and hair slough off, from head and flippers first. The new fur is a silvery gray, as gorgeous as samite. The dark spots that cover it are larger than before the molt. When the spotted female is fully mature, after two or three more molts, the dark spots will coalesce into the black saddle shapes that are the distinctive mark of her tribe.

The lethargy of the molt lifts from the seals, and they slide off the floes. In a jubilation of release, they hunt and surge through the sea. The insistent urge to move, to migrate, grips them again. They gather in pods of from twenty to thirty animals and swim toward the north and east.

The writer George Allan England saw the migrating seals in the 1920s and wrote, enchanted: "They flung up sheaves of foam that flashed in scattered rays of sunshine – swift, joyous forms that plunged, rolled and dived in dashing froth; Nature's supreme last word in vital force and loveliness and grace."

The harp seals eat a lot. The two million harp seals of the Gulf and Front herds consume each year about seven billion pounds of fish and crustaceans. Studies carried out by David Sergeant of the Arctic Biological Station show that sixty percent of their food is fish, and of the fish twenty percent are capelin.

The harp seal's great annual migration, five thousand miles through the trackless sea, doubles its food supply. In summer it hunts in the rich waters of the north, in winter in the even richer waters east and west of Newfoundland, on the Grand Banks

The pup is nearly fully molted; a few tufts of baby wool remain on its sides and flippers, and whitish fur still covers its face.

The fully molted harp seal pup in silvery-gray, dark-dappled fur is called a "beater."

and in the Gulf of St. Lawrence. John Davis, the Elizabethan explorer, caught there in 1586 "the largest and best fed fish that ever [he] sawe," and Sir Humphrey Gilbert visited Newfoundland in 1583 and wrote to his friend the historian Richard Hakluyt that on land "I see nothing but solitude... [but in the sea there is] an inexhaustible supply of fish." I rowed once across a fiord in Labrador and beneath me in serried ranks swam capelin, a steady stream of life nine miles across.

Once, capelin seemed inexhaustible. They fed the cod and the whales, the seals, the murres and the puffins. And there were plenty left for man to harvest in profligate abundance. In 1869 Capt. R.B. McCrea, in his book *Lost Amid the Fogs*, described a Newfoundland capelin scull, when the fish arrived in a "stupendous... multitude" and people ran into the surf and stood "up to their hips in fish and hauled them out in buckets." Everyone ate capelin, and "heaps upon heaps [were] spread over the fields for manure."

Capelin were the base of higher life at sea, essential to the sea's interdependent web of life. Yet Canada, in ignorance and folly, gave its capelin away to other nations, primarily to the Soviet Union, whose giant fleet scooped up the shoals of capelin and turned them into human food and into fish meal, protein-rich feed for pigs and chickens. The catch soared from 3,000 metric tons in 1970 to 370,000 metric tons in 1976. In a few years it was over. Capelin stocks crashed; seabirds perished; cod, deprived of their main prey, starved.

The decline of the capelin may also have affected the seals, but since humans are reluctant to admit their mistakes, the decline of the capelin was blamed on the seals and on the end of the seal hunt. Because the hunt has ceased, the argument goes, the seals have increased in number and have become a threat to the remaining capelin. Therefore the seal hunt will have to be resumed. But the public is not swayed by graphs and statistics, or by arguments for a "maximum sustainable yield." It remembers the images of cute white pups with large, trusting eyes, of men with long clubs, and of ice smeared with blood.

Newfoundland sealers also hunted the adult, molting seals, usually from boats. This was a risky hunt. The sealers left their ships in pairs, the "gunner" and his "dog," the helper who carried the heavy bag of ammunition. The men wore "skinnywoppers," knee-high sealskin boots, their soles studded with "sparables," sharp nails. They "copied" (jumped) skillfully from floe to floe. The air was filled with the crash and zing of bullets ricocheting off the ice. The ships zigzagged through the pack, retrieving shot seals left by the men.

At dusk the ships attempted to collect their scattered crews. When fog shrouded the floes and storms dispersed the pack, the men often perished on the shifting, disintegrating ice. More than a thousand Newfoundland sealers died and thousands more were crippled. The hunt of the molting seals was extremely wasteful. Unless the bullet shattered its head, the seal, with a final spasm, slid off the ice and sank into the sea. It is estimated that for every seal the sealers killed and got, they killed and lost another twenty.

Hunting in the deep, a harp seal has
grabbed a sculpin. Now it tries to rid itself
of the fish that cuts its mouth with needle-
sharp spines.

The hand-long polar cod is a main summer food of the harp seal in the Far North.

Following pages: Harp seals in the somber glow of the setting sun.

Despite their slow, heavy appearance, harp seals can be surprisingly quick. They rear up on strong front flippers for a better view, then undulate urgently across the ice toward water.

Wind drives the floes against the Magdalen Islands in the distance; they buckle and break and rise in pressure ridges.

Following pages: Harp seals are gregarious. They migrate in pods and like to be close to each other on the breeding ice. Yet each female has a private sphere which other seals may not enter.

Above: A pup begins to molt its pure-white natal fur.

Right: Sunrise over seals, ice floes and pressure ridges.

7
KAIRULIT: THE JUMPING SEALS

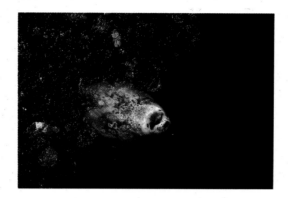

The night is calm and luminous; the sea is satin smooth: Icebergs float serenely in the water, soft rose and ivory yellow in the slanting rays of the midnight sun, cool green or steely blue in deep shadows. Ice pieces, carved by wind and waves into polished, shimmering shapes, are mirrored in the glowing sea. The seabirds feed. Arctic terns hover on beating wings, peer intently downward, dive and emerge with tiny fish held in scarlet stiletto beaks. A great concourse of murres mumbles among the ice floes. They have come from Agparssuit, north of Upernavik on the west coast of Greenland, a famous loomery where a million pairs of murres nest on the narrow ledges of sheer cliffs. They lie like dark toy birds upon the sea and dive suddenly with silvery splashes. Fat and laden with food, they race across the glossy sea to gain flying speed, leaving twin tracks that spread across the water.

A school of harp seals surfaces in happy confusion; they twist and turn and snort and leap. *Kairulit*, the jumping seals, Inuit call them. The spotted female is among this group of older seals; it is the first time she has been this far north.

The molted pups, the "beaters," cross Davis Strait and spend summer and fall in the fiords of southwest Greenland munching crustaceans, infinitely abundant and easy to catch. The immature seals, the "bedlamers," swim farther north and gorge on capelin. The adult harp seals travel farthest north, past Disko Bay and Upernavik, past the dark, jutting cliffs of the soaring mountain known as Djaevelens Tommelfinger, the Devil's Thumb, into Melville Bay, girt by alabaster cliffs, four hundred miles of glaciers. A few swim into the northernmost reaches of Baffin Bay. Many pods turn west and head for the channels, straits, sounds and inlets among the islands of Canada's high-arctic archipelago, to feed on polar cod and Greenland halibut, and upon those black pelagic snails which Polar Inuit call *tulugarssaq*, the ones that look like ravens. Although they are very numerous, the seals spread out over a sea area nearly as large as Western Europe, minimizing the pressure on the food resources of any one region.

A deadly shadow glides across the satin sea. The Inuk hunter hears the splashing seals and paddles his white-painted kayak with utmost caution; the blades cut smoothly

Above: The ringed seal is the smallest and most numerous of all northern seal species.

Left: Ice glitters beneath the midnight sun.

103

into the water and are lifted without the slightest splash. He hides behind ice floes and small bergs. The seals are still frolicking in the rose-tinted water of the night. The man eases his sleek kayak around a big floe. The seals are more than a hundred yards away, too far for a sure shot. But he knows they will dive any moment. He takes careful aim and fires. The crash shatters the arctic night. Murres patter frantically across the sea, the seals dive in wild confusion. The man paddles his kayak to the spot where they disappeared. Traces of fat and blood mark the roiled water. The hunter waits patiently, but the wounded seal is lost.

Beneath the surface, the frightened seals dive fast and deep. They call continuously, and gradually the scattered pod regroups. They swim underwater for nearly twenty minutes, twice as long as usual, and when they surface they are wary and afraid. The shot and the strange noises of the dying seal have frightened them. The older seals head west, away from the coast. The spotted female and her companions begin to cross Baffin Bay.

Inuit kayak hunters return to their camp along the Greenland coast.

A hunter waits patiently in a kayak for seals to surface within shooting range.

The wounded seal twists downward, trailing whorls and streaks of crimson blood through the greenish sea. The bullet tore into her chest just above the front flipper and mushroomed as it passed through her body, shredding her lungs and a major artery. She dived instinctively, seeking safety in the sea, but she is losing control. She struggles upward, but her flippers no longer respond. The body jerks and twists; the dying seal slides slowly toward the darkness of the deep.

From the deep, attracted by the smell of blood, comes the long gray shape of a shark, and from its large dead eyes dangle two white worms, immensely specialized parasitic copepods (*Ommatokoita elongata*) that live only on the eyes of Greenland sharks. The shark swims cautiously toward the sinking seal and touches it. The seal is dead. The great fish turns, the low-slung mouth opens wide, showing the lower teeth fused into a single, serrated razor-sharp blade of pearly white, and with one smooth motion it cuts a circular piece of skin, blubber and meat out of the seal. Slowly, methodically, the shark scoops out chunk after chunk, shearing off ten pounds

with every bite. The mangled remains of what was once a seal drift to the sea bottom and are soon covered by hordes of feeding shrimps and crabs.

Seals spread to the northern seas millions of years ago and became superbly adapted to the demands of this icy realm. The five most important seal species share the food-wealth of this region in noncompetitive fashion. The small ringed seal of the circumpolar seas feeds on polar cod and on swarms of shrimplike crustaceans, especially *Mysis* and *Parathemisto*, slurping them in like a rich and nourishing broth. The large bearded seal with long, droopy, sensitive whiskers scours the bottom of the sea for shrimps, octopods, flounders, Greenland halibut, crabs, cockles and holothurian worms. Its favorite food is whelks, which it somehow extracts from their whorled homes; it never swallows the shells. Harp seals harvest the upper layers of the sea. The big,

A hooded seal pup is called a "blueback" because its back fur is slaty blue.

dark hooded seals feed at greater depth on redfish, squid and cod. The fifth species, the walruses, grub along the ocean floor searching for shellfish; with their powerful, mobile lips, they suck up, on the average, three to four thousand clams a day.

To Inuit and polar bears, the seal was everything. For both it made arctic life possible. Two hundred and fifty thousand years ago, a mere instant in evolutionary time, brown bears in northern Siberia, descendants of Europe's giant cave bears, ventured beyond land and began to hunt seals upon the ice. Over countless generations their fur turned from brown to camouflage white, for on the ice selective pressure favored light-colored animals. They acquired an intimate knowledge of seal behavior, and they evolved into polar bears, highly specialized hunters of seals.

Man came last. Ancestors of the Inuit crossed Bering Strait ten thousand years ago and spread during millennia across the hostile but game-rich Arctic. With the exception of a few inland groups who lived primarily on caribou, the coastal Inuit were sea-mammal hunters. Once, long ago, I asked Inuterssuaq, a Polar Inuk with

whom I lived for many months, what is the most important thing in life. He reflected for a while, then smiled and said: "Seals, for without them we could not live."

Tents, in former days, were made of sealskins, as were pants and jackets so strong they lasted for years. Even now many Inuit wear sealskin boots, the shaft of soft ringed seal fur, the sole of extremely durable bearded seal leather. Seal meat and fat were the main food of the people and their sled dogs, and meals were cooked above semilunar soapstone lamps filled with seal oil. Murre eggs and greens were preserved in seal oil and kept reasonably fresh for more than a year. Today, when the people of Little Diomede Island in Bering Strait have to go to hospital, they usually take a large bottle of seal oil along because without it, they say, "food just doesn't taste right." Their boats, the sleek kayak and the large umiak, were covered with sealskins or with split walrus hide, and from the intestines of the bearded seal they made waterproof clothing, bags, and sails for their boats. Thong was cut in a spiral from bearded seal skin and used as sled dog traces, to lash the sled load, and as the essential line that connected the kayak hunter's harpoon with the *avatak*, the inflated sealskin float. Thimbles were made from bearded seal leather, and from the throat membrane of the hooded seal the Polar Inuit made the parchment of their drums. Bones were carved into children's toys, or into *ajagait*, skill-testing ring-and-pin games, and with the phalangeal bones of seals the Inuit played *inugaq*, a game akin to dice. Had the world been created with but one animal, the seal, the Inuit would have been content, for it gave them nearly everything they needed.

Above: A female hooded seal and a male with its hood inflated.

Right: The sole of a sealskin boot is made of thick, durable bearded seal leather. The seamstress chews the sole to make it pliable for sewing.

Preceding pages: An Inuk woman pegs the skins of ringed seals to the ground to dry. With these skins she will make the shafts of sealskin boots.

Unlike the usually timid harp seal mothers, the female hooded seal remains with her pup and defends it.

In addition to inflating its "hood," the skin
crest upon its head, the male hooded seal
can also extrude and inflate its nasal sep-
tum to impress the female and all rivals.

In summer, warmth, wind and waves carve
intricate patterns into the northern ice.

A female hooded seal watches an
approaching male. She mates a week to
ten days after giving birth to her pup.

8
WITH WALRUSES AND UNICORNS

The sound of delicate, distant bells rings softly through the arctic sea. A massive, warty walrus bull hangs vertically in the water and emits the sound of gentle chimes. His huge pharyngeal pouches act as resonators and magnify the sound.

This sea is full of noises the spotted seal has never heard before. She and her pod crossed Baffin Bay, feeding on polar cod and crustaceans, and now they have swum into Lancaster Sound, the entrance to the Northwest Passage, that Holy Grail of arctic exploration in whose quest so many arctic explorers died. It is also the richest, most diverse sea mammal region of Canada.

The walruses are noisy, chummy, messy and disputatious. They lie in madder-brown heaps upon the pristine floes, which they smear with their feces. They roar and bellow and threaten each other with gleaming ivory tusks. A bull swims around a floe packed with dozing walruses and clicks and clacks his teeth so rapidly it sounds like fast-played castanets.

Unlike the pelagic harp seals, which spend days and weeks in water, walruses haul out frequently and sleep in tight groups on land or on ice. In Lancaster Sound the ice floes that float conveniently above the rich shellfish beds where they feed are their diving platforms.

The spotted female and her group hear the noisy walruses from afar and avoid them. Most are harmless shellfish eaters, but about one in a thousand is a "killer," a rogue walrus that hunts and kills seals. A killer walrus lost its mother when it was very young. It survived by eating benthic worms and carrion, developed a taste for meat and began to kill and eat seals. Other walruses, normally compulsively gregarious, shun the rogue. He is the outcast of the tribe and travels and sleeps alone. He looks and smells different. His shoulders and forelimbs are exceptionally large and powerful. His chin, throat, chest and tusks are amber yellow, stained by the oxidized fat of the seals he has killed. His tusks, like ivory daggers, are long, slender and sharp. He swims silently up to a sleeping seal, enfolds it with powerful front flippers, crushes it, rips the skin with his tusks, holds the corpse and sucks off its blubber and some meat.

Above: A massive, warty walrus bull. Most walruses are shellfish eaters. About one in a thousand is a killer that kills and eats seals.

Left: Attracted by the smell of blood from a wounded seal, a Greenland shark swims into shallow water near the coast of northern Baffin Island.

The seals swim into Barrow Strait past the soaring brownish limestone cliffs of Prince Leopold Island, speckled with brooding murres and kittiwakes. The sea is full of sounds: the drawn-out, rising-falling trill of bearded seals, the yowls and chirps and puppy-yelps of ringed seals. Unlike the gregarious harp seals, which travel together in friendly, talkative pods and breed in close proximity upon the ice, bearded seals and ringed seals are usually loners. When ringed seals trespass upon each other's marine domain, they sometimes bark like angry dogs.

The harp seal pod follows an artificial lead created by an icebreaker bound for Resolute on Cornwallis Island. Deep bassoon notes swell through the sea, as well as rapid clicks and whistles, and from time to time a dry *click-clack* like wooden sticks beaten together. Narwhal are jousting in the lead. Dark-backed mottled males swim at each other. Each one carries a single, sinistrally spiraled, seven-foot-long ivory tusk, its tip polished and gleaming. Theirs is a stylized combat. The two-ton males glide above and below each other, cross tusks, turn tightly and face each other again – a strange underwater duel, but rarely a bloody one. The males do not transfix each other with their gleaming tusks, but he who has the longest tusk has probably the highest standing in the hierarchy of narwhal males.

In late August, while the seals are feeding off Somerset Island just past the tombolo and islet at the entrance to Cunningham Inlet where arctic terns nest and jaegers like to gather, the thousand white whales who spent the summer in the shallow, relatively warm waters of the inlet leave en masse, and the sea throbs with discordant voices, for these are the most vocal of all whales. They talk incessantly. Scientists catalogued several hundred separate sounds made by white whales before they nearly ran out of words and similes. The whales burp and chirp, croak, scream, squeak, grunt, trill, mew, moo and yap; they bellow like bulls and low like cattle, they whinny like horses and grunt like pigs, they cry like babies and they emit the piercing wolf-whistle of a seasoned lecher. In air one can hear them more than a mile away. In water their voices fill a bay, nearly drowning out the low talk of the seals.

One female whale carries an oval piece of driftwood on her back. Each time it slips, she dives, comes up beneath the wood and travels on with it. It is her baby. Her recently born calf died six days ago. Calves often ride on their mothers' broad backs and cling with short flippers and great tenacity to their gleaming white, rubber-smooth skins. When her calf died, the female supported its body and kept it at the surface in the life-giving air. On a stormy day she lost her calf and it slid to the bottom of the inlet. It was then she adopted the piece of driftwood; she carries it carefully and talks to it.

The days and nights are getting colder. On the last day of August a snowstorm whirls across land and sea, and snow remains on the hills. The birds fly south. At night a film of new, dark ice links the floes of yesteryear. The floes twist in current and in wind, and the thin ice crumples with a whisper. It re-forms the next night and binds the floes together. The food is copious, the living easy, but the seals are getting nervous. Except during their breeding season in the south, they are seals of the open sea.

Gregarious and talkative, white whales mill
in the shallow water of a high-arctic inlet.

After feeding on clams,
fat walruses sleep
soundly on an ice floe.

A pod of ivory-tusked
narwhals, the unicorns
of the arctic seas.

The harp seals swim east out of Lancaster Sound before the spreading ice bars their way. Near Cape Hay on Bylot Island a gigantic gray-black form swims slowly through the sea. The bowhead whale is feeding; its mouth, so cavernous it could hold an entire pod of seals, is open. From the bow-shaped upper jaw hang 350 closely spaced triangular baleen plates, up to fourteen feet in length. The whale scoops in water swarming with small crustaceans. From time to time the great mouth closes, the one-ton tongue moves up, water gushes through the latticework of baleen and the crustacean gruel that remains is swept back and swallowed, about a ton a day. Once there were thousands of bowheads in these seas but few survived a century of systematic slaughter. The great whale swims alone.

When Capt. William Edward Parry of Britain's Royal Navy sailed his two ships into Lancaster Sound in late July of 1819, he found an arctic Eden, "the headquarters of the whales." Schools of giant bowheads swam slowly through the sea. On July 30 they saw eighty-nine. Narwhal were "very numerous," and white whales "were swimming about the ships in great numbers."

Whalers followed the explorers and killed the fat, slow bowheads. And when the bowhead whales became scarce, the whalers killed all other sea mammals in this region. In 1883 they killed 2,736 white whales in Lancaster Sound and Baffin Bay. It was easy. Massed in favorite bays and inlets, the white whales were driven into shallow water, and Capt. William Adams reported that "when the tide recedes the white whales are left aground . . . and then the slaughter commences." In 1910 his crew killed more than seven hundred white whales in one inlet alone.

Attitudes changed. The bowhead of the eastern Arctic is protected now. The commercial hunting of white whales has ceased. Even the Russians, inveterate whale hunters, felt pity when in 1985 three thousand white whales were trapped by ice north of Siberia. They sent the icebreaker *Moskva* to free the animals but, reported Canadian scientist Maxwell J. Dunbar, "The shy whales would not follow their rescuers to safety, and the crew tried to lead them with music. Pop and martial music failed, but Wagner struck a responsive chord, and the whales followed the ship to the strains of *Tristan and Isolde*."

For the eastern Arctic bowhead population, protection came too late. Hunting ceased seventy years ago, yet in a sea area many times the size of France only two to four hundred of the great, slow-reproducing whales are left. Recently four eminent scientists of the Arctic Biological Station, Randall Reeves, Edward Mitchell, Arthur Mansfield and Michele McLaughlin, made a detailed study of the distribution of the bowhead whale in the eastern North American Arctic and ended their report on a sad note: "We can state that nothing we have seen in published accounts or in the unpublished records examined for this study inspires confidence in the population's ability to recover from overexploitation."

Left: Short flippers and a fat body make scratching difficult.

Preceding pages: The gregarious walruses usually travel in chummy pods.

Above: Females often threaten each other but rarely fight.

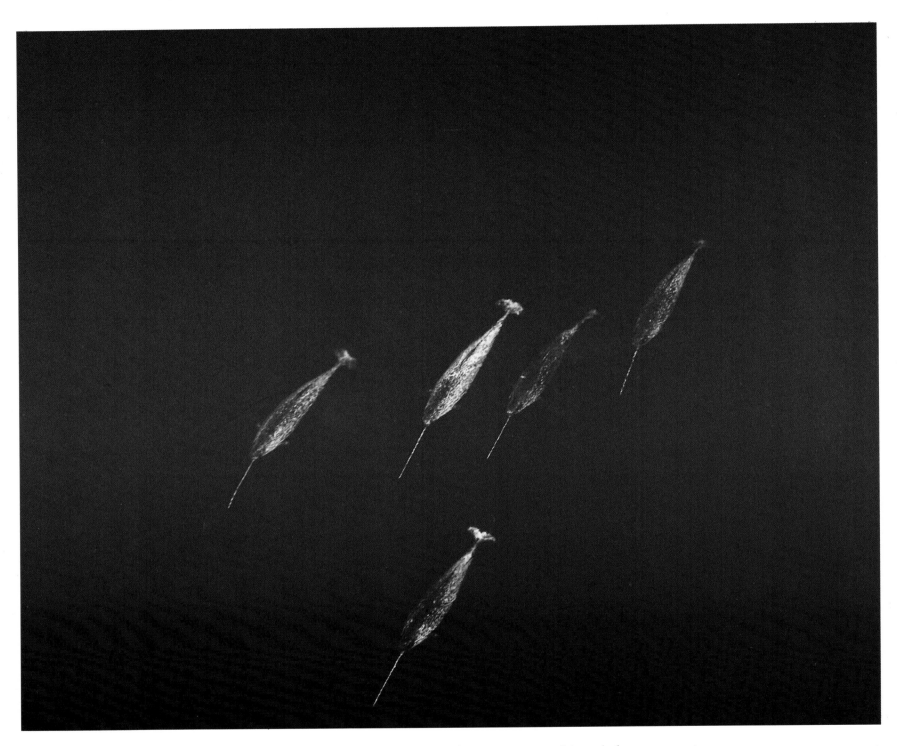

Above: Sleek and swift, ivory-tusked narwhal males glide through the dark water of Barrow Strait in the Canadian Arctic.

Preceding pages: A bearded seal near the northern coast of Greenland.

Right: In summer, white whales congregate near the estuaries of some arctic rivers.

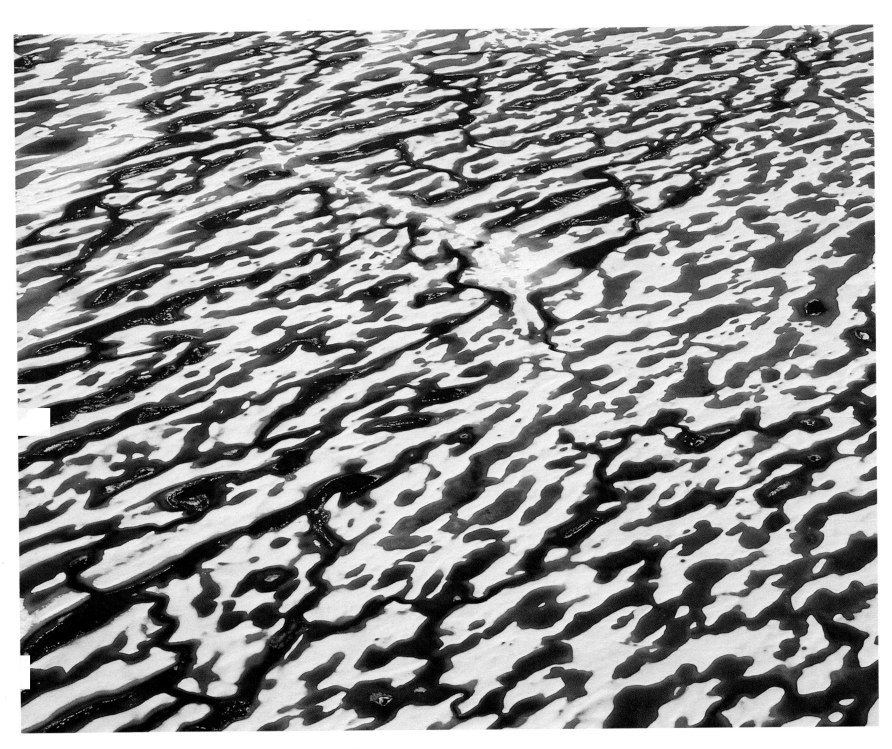

Summer ice in Lancaster Sound, seamed
by rifts and pools of dark water.

Its "hood" inflated, a male hooded seal
challenges another male.

9
DOWN THE ICY LABRADOR

T he seals swim through greenish waves of icy coruscating fire. Each seal is outlined in a phosphorescent glow and leaves a wake of pallid green. This is the autumnal flowering of the sea, a brief burst of life before the dormancy of winter. Dinoflagellates swarm through the dark water. In the marvelous laboratories of their microscopic bodies a substance known as luciferin combines with oxygen in the presence of the enzyme luciferase to produce a heatless pale green light. In their billions they crest each wavelet like liquid phosphorus and limn in lambent fire the creatures that rush through the sea.

The spotted seal and her companions swim just ahead of winter. They left Lancaster Sound in the first days of September, and one month and more than a thousand miles later they are off Cape Chidley in northernmost Labrador. The seals ride the currents. In summer they swam north in the warmish West Greenland Current, and now they return with the icy Labrador Current, a moving mass of water ten to twenty miles across and thirteen hundred feet deep that carries them south at a steady rate of half a mile an hour.

Lured by silvery clouds of fish, the seals swim into Hebron Fiord. They are now a scattered multitude, for many pods join in the southward migration. The seals feed avidly. Bunching fish are hard to catch, but when many seals scatter the shoals, the hunter's success in picking up one fish after another improves.

The nights are very cold. Pale green auroras flare across the velvet sky. The seals swim past the long-abandoned Inuit village on the north shore of the fiord, with its Moravian church built of massive oak pillars and beams brought from Germany in 1832. Not far from it is the rendering shed, where for more than a century seal blubber was rendered into oil, barreled and shipped to Europe. The decaying building still reeks with the rancid smell of ancient oil.

The wealth of fish and crustaceans draws the seals farther and farther up the fiord, and several hundred pursue their prey into the narrow-necked southern arm. And there the seals are trapped. Ice forms across the fiord, barring their exit to the open sea. The seals swim far beneath the ice and then return. The band is too broad.

Above: Return to the gulf. At the end of her southward migration, a female hooded seal swims among the ice floes in the Gulf of St. Lawrence.

Left: Hooded seals on the Gulf of St. Lawrence ice. A pale halo surrounding the sun usually presages a snowstorm.

The seals wait for many days, but no storm comes to break the ice. Then one day some of the older seals haul out on the ice; the companionship of many months is strong, and the spotted female follows them. They scrape and slither and slide across the polished ice, an anxious throng of vulnerable seals, all heading east, guided by "water sky," the dark reflection of distant open water upon the clouds. The belt of ice has grown to many miles. The seals, out of their element, hitch tiredly and awkwardly for nearly an entire day across the vast expanse until they reach the sea.

About a hundred seals remain behind. Some swim southwest, toward land. To their astigmatic vision the dark line of distant trees looks just like the dark line of open water. Some hump ashore on a snowy beach. Others creep onto the encroaching ice. Frantic and confused and rapidly weakening, the animals continue on and on, until their skin wears through and pink tracks mark the path of the doomed seals. "Crawlers," they call them in Labrador.

The saved seals idle down the coast. The moving water of the current does not

On a cold day, water droplets beading a female's whiskers turn to ice in a few moments.

freeze, the food is ample, the seals have lots of time. They pass Cape Porcupine, called Kjølneset (Keel Point) by the exploring Vikings who found there a thousand years ago the remnants of a ship, and miles and miles of yellow sand, the Wonder Beaches of this rocky land, the "Furdurstrandir" of the Norsemen.

The seals swim through a deep gut between two islands. The spotted female veers to chase a fish, and something grabs and holds her flipper. She spins immediately to free herself, 350 pounds of frightened seal, and the torqued nylon thread cuts deeply into her skin. She jerks and twists and turns. Only one mesh near the edge of the net holds her; it breaks and she is free. She dives deep and rushes away, calling to her companions.

Two of her group are dying in the net. They swam into the large-meshed seal net near its center, and it enfolds them. The more they thrash and turn in desperation, the tighter the mesh twists around their struggling bodies. Their entire beings throb with the terrible need for air, and slowly, slowly, they die.

Labrador, said the Elizabethan explorer John Davis in 1586, is a country of "fayre woods and of foule and fishe mighty store."

The later settlers of Labrador called the migrating harps the "voyage seals." The Labrador trader Lambert De Boilieu saw them in the 1850s: "To mark a shoal of these animals . . . quietly swimming, with head and part of the shoulder out of the water – the head, by the way, being a jetty black, and the shoulders tinged with a silver lustre – the coal-black eye shining at a distance like a diamond, is a magnificent sight indeed. I have often, I must own, felt remorse when killing these animals, there is such a human expressiveness in their eye, in fact in their entire visage." And, De Boilieu adds, "this kind of seal produces about ten gallons of oil."

As the seals descended the Labrador coast, the Inuit hunted them with kayaks or nets, the European settlers mainly with nets. The naturalist Alpheus S. Packard watched Inuit in the 1880s hunt seals at minus twenty degrees Fahrenheit. "In this temperature the Eskimo sits for hours at a time, bound fast in his kayak . . . wet through by the

Sleek and soundless, Inuit kayaks glide across the northern sea.

A harp seal mother in the soft light of evening.

icy spray of the waves, which at once freeze on his skiff and on his clothes." And every morning and every night, drenched by freezing spray, the men hauled up the heavy nets.

On July 23, 1833, John James Audubon in southern Labrador visited "the Seal establishment of a Scotchman, Samuel Robertson. . . . His seal-oil tubs were full and he was then engaged in loading two schooners for Quebec with that article." In good years, the Robertsons took two to three thousand migrating harp seals in their nets.

This ancient and efficient method of catching harp seals may now end. In 1986 a Royal Commission on Seals and the Sealing Industry in Canada recommended: "In view of the suffering involved, the government should take action with a view to phasing out, as rapidly as possible, the netting of seals in those communities which now rely largely on this method to take harp seals both for subsistence and to provide a substantial part of their income. Netting of seals in other areas should be prohibited immediately."

Hooded seals on the
polished ice at the
approach of night.

A large-eyed shape near the surface, a seal
mother stares at the human who has
invaded her icy realm.

In a drifting world of ice, the females surface in leads frequently.

Following pages: The seal's body, with its sleek shape and layers of fat, is well suited to life in icy water.

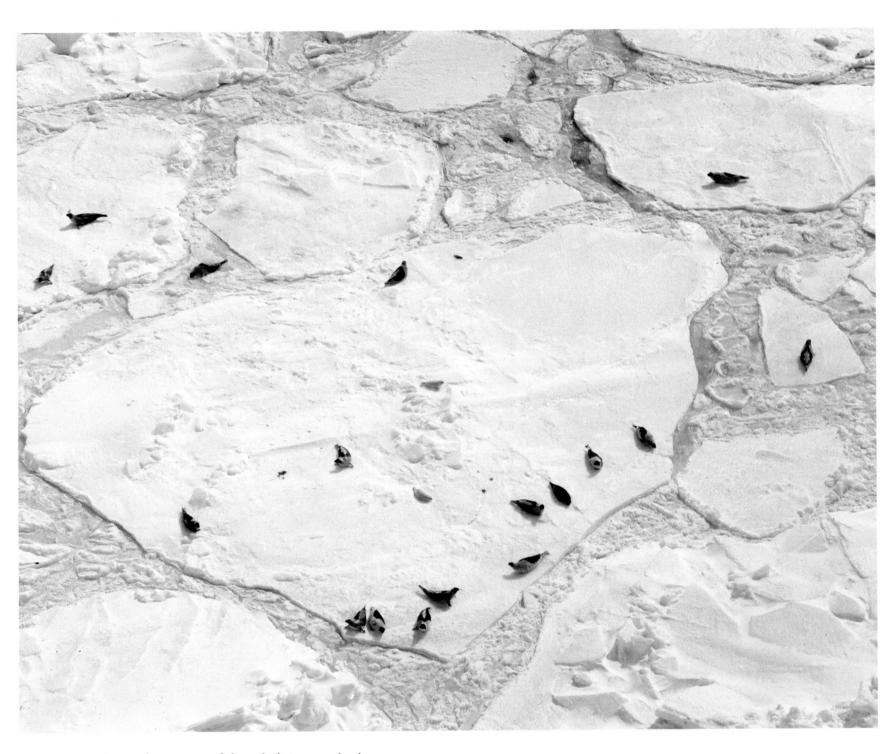

Near the center of the whelping patch, the
females lie closely spaced on the ice.

After a five-thousand-mile migration,
the harp seals return to the Gulf of
St. Lawrence in January.

10
RETURN TO THE GULF

The seals have swum five thousand miles. Of all the annual pinniped migrations, only that of the northern fur seal, which breeds on islands in the Bering Sea and winters off California, is longer (by perhaps a thousand miles).

Near the Strait of Belle Isle in late December the harp seal throng, a multitude of many chummy pods, divides again into separate herds. The spotted seal and her companions met nearly randomly during the spring-summer migration. They swam together, fed together and knew each other's voices. At the Strait of Belle Isle a much more ancient bond and call asserts itself.

The harp seals that were born on the Front continue to swim south-southeast. They will winter in the region of the Grand Banks, and two months hence the gravid females will seek out the immensity of the floating pack, 25,000 square miles of ice, and give birth upon the drifting floes.

The spotted female and the other seals born in the gulf branch off from their summer companions and swim southwest into the Strait of Belle Isle, compelled by an ancient command, triggered, perhaps, by a change in the water's salinity, a change in its taste, a strangely familiar feeling.

The sea steams. It is intensely cold. Gray wisps of steam shiver in the icy air above a sullen sea. Ice crystals form in the rapidly cooling water, drift to the surface as frazil ice, and the sea becomes sluggish and leaden. A pale yellow sun hangs above the horizon, flanked by paler mock suns. "Sun hounds," they call them in Newfoundland and believe they presage storms, those "dismal gales," as Audubon said, "which blow ever and anon over this desolate country ... [and whose] horrid blasts seem strong enough to rend the very rocks asunder."

The seals no longer form merry pods that jump and frolic and play. A hundred thousand pregnant females search for ice. The spotted female swims with them obliquely southwestward across the gulf, past the rust-red walls of the Bird Rock.

West of the Magdalen Islands the great flat pans begin to form. With her long sharp nails, the spotted female scrapes a hole into the ice. She returns regularly to this hole to breathe, and when other seals approach she warns them away.

Above: Meltwater covers the ice and soaks a pup's fur. The seal's thick blubber layer protects it from the sapping chill of the water.

Left: A female surfaces in her bobbing hole.

147

In late February the ice is nearly two feet thick. The female scrapes the ice until her hole is big enough for her to haul out. It is now a "bobbing hole," as Newfoundlanders say. The female lies upon the ice beneath a wan and wintry sun. All around and far away the ice is speckled with the shapes of seals, one hundred thousand females who will give birth within the next few days.

The presence of other seals reassures the spotted female. Yet when one of them surfaces in her bobbing hole, she arches her body and threatens the seal with a high-pitched gurgling trill. She is tense and edgy. She sleeps, flat and flaccid, upon the ice,

On the jumbled ice blocks of a pressure ridge, a female harp seal rears up in her threat posture.

Harp seals never touch land. Pups are born on the ice, seals haul out onto the ice to molt and spend the rest of the year at sea.

wakes, turns, hitches herself laboriously back and forth on the ice, argues with a neighboring female, scratches the ice with a flailing front flipper and trills her warning. Then she humps to her bobbing hole and peers into the sea where other seals glide through the water with graceful ease, hauls her heavy body back across the ice, slumps and sleeps for a while.

In the morning, an hour before sunrise, the spotted female twists and groans. She stretches, twists again. Suddenly she raises her abdomen off the ice, her hind flippers flare, and with one violent contraction she expels the pup from her body. It

glides upon the ice, a steaming parcel of life wrapped in a gleaming membrane.

The female turns sharply and with one abrupt twist breaks the umbilical cord. She nuzzles the pup, breaks the caul and inhales deeply its specific scent. Henceforth she will know by smell her pup from all the other pups born on the ice.

The newborn pup stirs feebly. Its head is big, its body thin, its fur yellow, wet and matted. It tries to lift its heavy head with little spastic twitches, and it cries, pathetic bleats that tell of hunger and of fear.

The spotted female rolls on her side. The pup instinctively knows that somewhere along the great dark form is the source of the milk it so desperately needs, but it does not know where. It drags itself with an enormous effort to the female and nuzzles her neck, her flipper, her shoulder. It shivers in violent spasms and becomes more frantic with every passing minute. It cries, and bubbly saliva trickles from its searching mouth.

Harp seal milk is creamy-rich. It contains forty-two percent fat and eleven percent protein.

Newborn pups are puzzled and curious when a human approaches. Older pups snarl and lunge.

Finally the mother helps. She moves her front flipper rapidly, shooing the pup away from her upper body toward the abdomen where the two teats lie hidden in skin folds beneath the fur. The pup searches and sucks and cries. At last, guided by a faint smell and the slightly warmer skin near the nipples, it finds the right spot and suckles strongly. The warm milk is wonderfully rich and creamy. The pup nurses eagerly, its eyes closed in blissful concentration. Finally full, it lies close to its mother, blinks a few times and falls asleep.

Most pups are born during the night, many just before morning. The day is cold and calm and clear. The sun rises and flecks the ice with nacre and gold. The air is full of the eager and anxious cries of just-born pups. The immense ice plains of the gulf are once again covered with new life, as they have been, year after year, for thousands of seal generations.

Preceding pages: A firm floe surrounded
by pressure ridges is crowded with harp
seal mothers and their pups.

Leads zigzag through the ice. A mother
seal returns to her pup.

A pup lies near its mother, a young female
whose saddle mark is still very faint.

A worried pup snarls at an intruder.

A spotted female and her three-day-old
pup on the rugged Front ice off southern
Labrador.

After its first swim, a pup hauls out onto the ice where it was born.

Water fascinates the pups, but they also fear it and at first are frantic when they fall in.

If cautiously approached, the pups are merely curious. If touched, they may defend themselves with flailing, sharp-clawed flippers.